TO

_____

FROM

_____

DATE

_____

HIS PASSION...

YOUR PURPOSE

The quoted ideas expressed in this book (but not scripture verses) are not, in all cases, exact quotations, as some have been edited for clarity and brevity. In all cases, the author has attempted to maintain the speaker's original intent. In some cases, quoted material for this book was obtained from secondary sources, primarily print media. While every effort was made to ensure the accuracy of these sources, the accuracy cannot be guaranteed. For additions, deletions, corrections or clarifications in future editions of this text, please write FAMILY CHRISTIAN PRESS.

Scripture quotations are taken from:

The Holy Bible, King James Version

The Holy Bible, New International Version (NIV) Copyright © 1973, 1978, 1984, by International Bible Society. Used by permission of Zondervan Publishing House. All rights reserved.

The Holy Bible, New King James Version (NKJV) Copyright © 1982 by Thomas Nelson, Inc. Used by permission.

The New American Standard Bible®, (NASB) Copyright © 1960, 1962, 1963, 1968, 1971, 1972, 1973, 1975, 1977, 1995 by The Lockman Foundation. Used by permission.

The Holy Bible, New Living Translation, (NLT) Copyright © 1996. Used by permission of Tyndale House Publishers, Inc., Wheaton, Illinois 60189. All rights reserved.

New Century Version®. (NCV) Copyright © 1987, 1988, 1991 by Word Publishing, a division of Thomas Nelson, Inc. All rights reserved. Used by permission.

The Message (MSG)- This edition issued by contractual arrangement with NavPress, a division of The Navigators, U.S.A. Originally published by NavPress in English as THE MESSAGE: The Bible in Contemporary Language copyright 2002-2003 by Eugene Peterson. All rights reserved.

Revised Standard Version. (RSV) Copyright © 1946, 1952, 1959, 1973 by the Division of Christian Education of the National Council of the Churches of Christ in the United States of America. All rights reserved. Used by permission.

The Holman Christian Standard Bible™ (HCSB) Copyright © 1999, 2000, 2001 by Holman Bible Publishers. Used by permission.

International Children's Bible®, New Century Version®. (ICB) Copyright © 1986, 1988, 1999 by Tommy Nelson™, a division of Thomas Nelson, Inc. All rights reserved. Used by permission.

Cover Design by Kim Russell / Wahoo Designs
Page Layout by Bart Dawson

ISBN 1-58334-240-0

TABLE OF CONTENTS

INTRODUCTION

To whom also he shewed himself alive after
his passion by many infallible proofs,
being seen of them forty days,
and speaking of the things pertaining
to the kingdom of God

Acts 1:3-5 *KJV*

O n a hill at Calvary, Jesus was crucified. Darkness came over the land, the curtain of the temple was torn in two, and finally Jesus called out, "Father, into your hands I commit my spirit" (Luke 23:46 NIV). Christ had endured the crucifixion.

The body of Jesus was wrapped in a linen shroud and placed in a new tomb. It was there that God breathed life into His Son. It was there that Christ was resurrected. It was there that the angels rejoiced. And it was there that God's plan for the salvation of mankind was to be made complete.

In the first chapter of Acts, we read that Jesus showed Himself to His followers "after his passion" (KJV). In this verse, the word passion refers to the suffering that Christ endured on the cross. Christ willingly endured that suffering so that we, His believers, might have life abundant *and* eternal. This text contains 31 devotional readings intended to assist you as you consider Christ's sacrifice and what that sacrifice means to you.

During the next 31 days, please try this experiment: read a chapter each day. If you're already committed to a daily time of worship, this book will enrich that experience. If you are not, the simple act of giving God a few minutes each morning will change the direction and the quality of your life.

God has a plan for everything, including you. As a part of that plan, He intends that you experience His love *and* His peace in this life *and* throughout all eternity. But perhaps your vision of God's plan is not quite as clear as you would like. If so, many of the ideas on these pages can help you discover God's purpose for your life.

If you genuinely seek God's guidance, He will give it. But, He will make His revelations known to you in a way and in a time of His choosing, not yours. So, if you're seeking to know God's will for your life, don't be worried if you haven't yet received a "final" answer. The final answer, of course, will come not in this world, but in the next. In the meantime, keep watching for God's signs and studying God's Word. When you sincerely seek His will—and *keep* seeking it—He will direct your path to a place of joyful abundance and eternal peace.

HIS PASSION

*But God demonstrates His own love toward us,
in that while we were still sinners,
Christ died for us.*

Romans 5:8 NKJV

Why did Christ go willingly to the cross at Calvary? Why did He choose to endure the "passion" (i.e. the suffering) that Luke describes in Acts 1:3? Why did the Son of God accept the humiliation and torture of the crucifixion? The answer is profoundly simple: He did it for you.

Christ humbled Himself on a cross—for you. He shed His blood—for you. He suffered and He died—for you. And now, Jesus offers to walk with you through this life *and* throughout all eternity.

The 19th-century writer Hannah Whitall Smith observed, "The crucial question for each of us is this: What do you think of Jesus, and do you yet have a personal acquaintance with Him?" Indeed, the answer to that question determines the quality, the course, and the direction of our lives today and for all eternity.

What should the passion of Christ mean to you? If you have been touched and transformed by His grace, then the passion of Christ should serve as a lens through which you view your life, your world, your purpose, your future, and your eternal destiny. So today, as you consider Christ's sacrifice on the cross, accept His love, praise His name, and share His message of salvation. And then, as you go about the duties of everyday life, conduct yourself in a manner that demonstrates to all the world that your acquaintance with the Master is not a passing fancy but that it is, instead, the cornerstone and the touchstone of your life.

The cross is the focus of all human history.

C. H. Spurgeon

To endure the cross is not tragedy;
it is the suffering which is the fruit
of an exclusive allegiance to Jesus Christ.

Dietrich Bonhoeffer

The cross is a tragedy to man,
but a tremendous triumph to God,
an absolute triumph.

Oswald Chambers

Who shall separate us from the love of Christ?
Shall tribulation, or distress, or persecution,
or famine, or nakedness, or peril, or sword?
Yet in all these things we are more than
conquerors through Him who loved us.

Romans 8:35, 37 NKJV

—A Prayer—

Dear Jesus, You are my Savior and my protector.
You suffered on the cross for me, and I will give
You honor and praise every day of my life.
I will honor You with my words, my thoughts,
and my prayers. And I will live according to
Your commandments, so that thorough me,
others might come to know Your perfect love.

—Amen—

Additional verses to consider

John 19:28-30; Romans 5:6; 1 Peter 3:18;
John 5:24; Ephesians 2:8

YOUR PURPOSE . . . AND GOD'S

*We know that all things work together
for the good of those who love God:
those who are called according to His purpose.*

Romans 8:28 HCSB

L ife is best lived on purpose, not by accident: the sooner we discover what God intends for us to do with our lives, the better. But God's purposes aren't always clear to us. Sometimes we wander aimlessly in a wilderness of our own making. And sometimes, we struggle mightily *against* God in a vain effort to find success and happiness through our own means, not His.

Whenever we struggle against God's plans, we suffer. When we resist God's calling, our efforts bear little fruit. Our best strategy, therefore, is to seek God's wisdom and to follow Him wherever He chooses to lead. When we do so, we are blessed.

When we align ourselves with God's purposes, we avail ourselves of His power and His peace. But how can we know precisely what God's intentions are? The answer, of course, is that even the most well-intentioned believers face periods of uncertainty and doubt about the direction of their lives. So, too, will you.

When you arrive at one of life's inevitable crossroads, that is precisely the moment when you should turn your thoughts and prayers toward God. When you do, He will make Himself known to you in a time and manner of His choosing.

Are you earnestly seeking to discern God's purpose for your life? If so, these pages are intended as a reminder of several important facts: 1. God has a plan for your life; 2. If you seek that plan sincerely and prayerfully, you will find it; 3. When you discover God's purpose for your life, you will experience abundance, peace, joy, and power—God's power. And that's the only kind of power that really matters.

You cannot fulfill God's purposes for your life while focusing on your own plans.

Rick Warren

Blessed are those who know what on earth they are here on earth to do and set themselves about the business of doing it.

Max Lucado

Oh Lord, let me not live to be useless.

John Wesley

*May He grant you according to your heart's desire,
and fulfill all your purpose.*

Psalm 20:4 NKJV

—A PRAYER—

Dear Lord, I know that You have a purpose
for my life, and I will seek that purpose today
and every day that I live. Let my actions be
pleasing to You, and let me share Your Good
News with a world that so desperately needs
Your healing hand and the salvation
of Your Son.

—Amen—

ADDITIONAL VERSES TO CONSIDER

*Ecclesiastes 3:1; Ephesians 4:1;
Philippians 3:13, 14; Psalm 16:11;
Romans 12:6-8*

As We Consider the Cross

Therefore we also, since we are surrounded by so great a cloud of witnesses, let us lay aside every weight, and the sin which so easily ensnares us, and let us run with endurance the race that is set before us, looking unto Jesus, the author and finisher of our faith, who for the joy that was set before Him endured the cross, despising the shame, and has sat down at the right hand of the throne of God.

Hebrews 12:1, 2 *NKJV*

As we consider the sacrifice that Jesus made upon the cross, we should be profoundly grateful and profoundly humbled. And today, as we come to Christ in prayer, we should do so in a spirit of quiet, heartfelt devotion to the One who gave His life so that we might have life eternal.

He was the Son of God, but He wore a crown of thorns. He was the Savior of mankind, yet He was put to death on rough-hewn cross made of wood. He offered His healing touch to an unsaved world, and yet the same hands that had healed the sick and raised the dead were pierced with nails.

Christ humbled Himself on a cross—for you. He shed His blood—for you. He has offered to walk with you through this life and throughout all eternity. As you approach Him today in prayer, think about His sacrifice and His grace. And be humble.

The spectacle of the Cross, the most public
event of Jesus' life, reveals the vast difference
between a god who proves himself
through power and One who proves
himself through love.

Philip Yancey

Forgiveness is the divine miracle of grace;
it cost God the Cross of Jesus Christ before
he could forgive sin and remain a holy God.

Oswald Chambers

Choose Jesus Christ! Deny yourself, take up
the Cross, and follow Him—for the world
must be shown. The world must see, in us,
a discernible, visible, startling difference.

Elisabeth Elliot

To accept Christ is to know the meaning of
the words "as he is, so are we in this world."
We accept his friends as our friends, his enemies
as our enemies, his ways as our ways,
his rejection as our rejection,
his cross as our cross, his life as our life,
and his future as our future.

A. W. Tozer

And being found in appearance as a man,
he humbled himself and became obedient
to death—even death on a cross!

Philippians 2:8 NIV

—A PRAYER—

Dear Lord, You sent Your Son Jesus to die on
a cross for me. Jesus endured indignity, suffering,
and death so that I might live. Because He lives,
I, too, have Your promise of eternal life.
Let me share this Good News, Lord,
with a world that so desperately needs
Your healing hand and the salvation of
Your Son. Today, let me share the message
of Jesus Christ through my words and my deeds.
—Amen—

ADDITIONAL VERSES TO CONSIDER

Romans 5:10; Philippians 2:5-8; Romans 6:4;
John 19:28-30

DISCOVERING PURPOSE DAY BY DAY

*I must work the works of Him who sent Me
while it is day; the night is coming
when no one can work.*

John 9:4 NKJV

God's purpose for your life unfolds day by day. Each new morning offers fresh opportunities to study God's Word and seek His will. That's why it is vitally important that you take time for a daily chat with God. No habit is more important to your spiritual health than the discipline of daily prayer and devotion to your Creator.

The words of John 9:4 remind us that "night is coming" for all of us. But until then, God gives us each day and fills it to the brim with possibilities. The day is presented to us fresh and clean at midnight, free of charge, but we must beware: Today is a non-renewable resource—once it's gone, it's gone forever. Our responsibility, of course, is to use this day in the service of God's will and in accordance with His commandments.

Today, treasure the time that God has given you. And search for the hidden possibilities that God has placed along your path. This day, like every other day, is a priceless gift from your Creator, so use it joyfully and productively. And encourage others to do likewise. After all, night is coming when no one can work . . .

Knowing God involves an intimate,
personal relationship that is developed
over time through prayer and getting answers
to prayer, through Bible study and applying its
teaching to our lives, through obedience
and experiencing the power of God,
through moment-by-moment submission to
Him that results in a moment-by-moment
filling of the Holy Spirit.

Anne Graham Lotz

With each new dawn, life delivers a package
to your front door, rings your doorbell, and runs.

Charles Swindoll

A man can no more take in a supply of grace
for the future than he can eat enough for
the next six months, or take sufficient air into
his lungs at one time to sustain life for a week.
We must draw upon God's boundless store of
grace from day to day as we need it.

D. L. Moody

Give your entire attention to what God is doing right now, and don't get worked up about what may or may not happen tomorrow. God will help you deal with whatever hard things come up when the time comes.

Matthew 6:34 MSG

—A PRAYER—

Lord, You have given me another day of life; let me celebrate this day, and let me use it according to Your plan. I praise You, Father, for my life and for the friends and family members who make it rich. Enable me to live each moment to the fullest as I give thanks for Your creation, for Your love, and for Your Son.

—Amen—

ADDITIONAL VERSES TO CONSIDER

Psalm 118:24; Hebrews 3:13; 2 Timothy 1:12; 2 Corinthians 6:2

PRIORITIES THAT ARE PLEASING TO GOD

Now it happened as they went that He entered
a certain village; and a certain woman named
Martha welcomed Him into her house. And she had
a sister called Mary, who also sat at Jesus' feet and
heard His word. But Martha was distracted with
much serving, and she approached Him and said,
"Lord, do You not care that my sister has left me
to serve alone? Therefore tell her to help me." And
Jesus answered and said to her, "Martha, Martha,
you are worried and troubled about many things.
But one thing is needed, and Mary has chosen that
good part, which will not be taken away from her."

Luke 10:38-42 NKJV

On your daily to-do list, all items are not created equal: Certain tasks are extremely important while others are not. Therefore, it's imperative that you prioritize your daily activities and complete each task in the approximate order of its importance.

The principle of doing first things first is simple in theory but more complicated in practice. Well-meaning family, friends, and coworkers have a way of making unexpected demands upon your time. Furthermore, each day has it own share of minor emergencies; these urgent matters tend to draw your attention away from more important ones. On paper, prioritizing is simple, but to act upon those priorities in the real world requires maturity, patience, determination, and balance.

If you're having trouble balancing the many demands of everyday living, perhaps you've been trying to organize your life according to your own plans, not God's. A better strategy, of course, is to take your daily obligations and place them in the hands of the One who created you. To do so, you must prioritize your day according to God's commandments, and you must seek His will and His wisdom in all matters. Then, you can face the coming day with the assurance that the same God who created our universe out of nothingness will help you place first things first in your own life.

The manifold rewards of a serious, consistent prayer life demonstrate clearly that time with our Lord should be our first priority.

Shirley Dobson

No test of a man's true character is more conclusive than how he spends his time and his money.

Patrick Morley

Have you prayed about your resources lately? Find out how God wants you to use your time and your money. No matter what it costs, forsake all that is not of God.

Kay Arthur

*The thing you should want most is God's kingdom
and doing what God wants. Then all these other
things you need will be given to you.*

Matthew 6:33 NCV

—A PRAYER—

Lord, let Your priorities be my priorities.
Let Your will be my will. Let Your Word
be my guide, and let me grow in faith
and in wisdom this day and every day.
—Amen—

ADDITIONAL VERSES TO CONSIDER

*1 Corinthians 9:24, 25; Hebrews 12:2;
Luke 9:23, 24; Philippians 3:15, 16;
Philippians 4:8, 9*

DEMANDS,
EXPECTATIONS,
AND
RESPONSIBILITIES

*So then each of us shall
give account of himself to God.*

Romans 14:12 NKJV

Expectations, expectations, expectations! As a dues-paying citizen of the 21st century, you know that demands can be high, and expectations even higher. The media delivers an endless stream of messages that tell you how to behave, how to eat, how to dress, and what to drive. The media's expectations are impossible to meet. God's are not. God doesn't expect you to be perfect . . . and neither should you.

The difference between perfectionism and realistic expectations is the difference between a life of frustration and a life of satisfaction. Only one earthly being ever lived life to perfection, and He was the Son of God. The rest of us have fallen short of God's standard and need to be accepting of our own limitations as well as the limitations of others.

If you find yourself frustrated by the unrealistic demands of others (or by unrealistic pressures of the self-imposed variety) it's time to ask yourself who you're trying to impress, and why. If you're trying to keep up with the Joneses, it's time to reconsider your priorities. Your first responsibility is to the heavenly Father who created you and to the Son who saved you. Then, you bear a powerful responsibility to be true to yourself. Furthermore, you owe your thanks and your love to beloved friends and family members. But, when it comes to meeting the unrealistic expectations of the media or the insatiable demands of the Joneses, forget it! After all, pleasing God is simply a matter of obeying His commandments and accepting His Son. But pleasing the Joneses? That's impossible!

Our responsibility is to feed from Him,
to stay close to Him, to follow Him—because
sheep easily go astray—so that we eternally
experience the protection and companionship
of our Great Shepherd the Lord Jesus Christ.

Franklin Graham

Freedom is not an absence of responsibility;
but rather a reward we receive when we've
performed our responsibility with excellence.

Charles Swindoll

Action springs not from thought,
but from a readiness for responsibility.

Dietrich Bonhoeffer

*The plans of the diligent lead to profit as surely as
haste leads to poverty.*

Proverbs 21:5 NIV

—A PRAYER—

Lord, help me to live up to Your expectations,
not the world's expectations. Let me seek
Your will and follow Your path, not a path that
is chosen for me by others. Your way is the right
path for me. And when I follow You, Father,
I will better serve my family, my friends,
my neighbors, and the world.

—*Amen*—

ADDITIONAL VERSES TO CONSIDER

Ezekiel 18:30; Revelation 2:23; Psalm 119:33;
1 Corinthians 4:3, 4

DISCOVERING PURPOSE THROUGH FAMILY AND FRIENDS

*You must choose for yourselves today
whom you will serve . . . as for me and my family,
we will serve the Lord.*

Joshua 24:15 NCV

As you consider God's purpose for your own life, you must also consider how your plans will effect the most important people that God has entrusted to your care: your loved ones.

Our families and friends are precious gifts from our Father in heaven. If we are to be worthy disciples of the One from Galilee, we must care for our loved ones and make time for them, even when the demands of the day are great. In a world filled with countless obligations and frequent frustrations, we may be tempted to take our families and friends for granted. But God intends otherwise. God intends that we honor Him by honoring our loved ones—by giving them our support, our time, and our cooperation.

No relationships are perfect, and neither are yours. Yet, imperfect though they may be, your family and friends are God's blessing to you. Give thanks for that blessing . . . and act accordingly.

We discover our role in life through
our relationships with others.

Rick Warren

With resolve that you are going to make
a relationship work, you can develop peace
treaties of love and tolerance and harmony
to transform a difficult situation
into something beautiful.

Max Lucado

I don't buy the cliché that quality time is
the most important thing. If you don't
have enough quantity, you won't get quality.

Leighton Ford

Line by line, moment by moment, special times
are etched into our memories in the permanent
ink of everlasting love in our relationships.

Gloria Gaither

A man's counsel is sweet to his friend.

Proverbs 27:9 NASB

—A PRAYER—

Dear Lord, You have given me a wonderful gift:
my loved ones. I thank You, Father,
for my family and friends. Today and
every day, let me show them that I love them by
the things that I say and the things that I do.

—Amen—

ADDITIONAL VERSES TO CONSIDER

*1 John 4:11; Proverbs 17:17; Romans 12:9, 10;
Proverbs 11:29; Matthew 12:25*

DISCOVERING PURPOSE IN THE WORKPLACE

*But thanks be to God, who gives us the victory
through our Lord Jesus Christ. Therefore,
my beloved brethren, be steadfast, immovable,
always abounding in the work of the Lord,
knowing that your labor is not in vain in the Lord.*

1 Corinthians 15:57, 58 NKJV

I f you've found work that you love, and if, through your efforts, you help make the world a better place, consider yourself doubly blessed. But, if you're dissatisfied with your employment, or if you feel that your professional life is not pleasing to God, then there's only one thing to do: you must keep searching.

Perhaps you've been searching for work that is pleasing to other people. Or perhaps you find yourself struggling in a job that is not suited to your skills. In either case, you must remember that God made you exactly as you are, and He did so for a very good reason: His reason. Therefore, you must glorify God by honoring the talents that He gave you, not the talents that you wish He had given you.

When you discover the work for which God created you, you'll be productive and inspired. But until you find that work, you'll have trouble generating enthusiasm. Unfortunately, too many of us have become intensely passionate about the things that improve neither the world nor ourselves.

Have you found a life's work about which you are passionate? Have you discovered a vocation that inspires you to arrive at the office ten minutes early rather than ten minutes late? Does your work help to create a better world *and* a better you? If the answer to these questions is yes, then consider yourself both fortunate and wise. But if the dream of meaningful work remains elusive, keep searching—and praying—until you find it.

Ordinary work, which is what most of us do most of the time, is ordained by God every bit as much as is the extraordinary.

Elisabeth Elliot

"They that sow bountifully shall reap also bountifully," is as true in spiritual things as in material.

Lottie Moon

The world does not consider labor a blessing, therefore it flees and hates it, but the pious who fear the Lord labor with a ready and cheerful heart, for they know God's command, and they acknowledge His calling.

Martin Luther

*Each will receive his own reward according
to his own labor. Each man's work
will become evident.*

1 Corinthians 3:8,13 NASB

—A PRAYER—

Dear Lord, make my work pleasing to You.
Help me to sow the seeds of Your abundance
everywhere I go. Let me be passionate in
all my undertakings and give me patience
to wait for Your harvest.

—Amen—

ADDITIONAL VERSES TO CONSIDER

1 Thessalonians 4:11, 12; 1 Timothy 5:8;
2 Chronicles 15:7; 2 Corinthians 9:6;
Colossians 3:23

CHANGING LIVES, OUR UNCHANGING GOD

Jesus Christ is the same yesterday,
today, and forever.

Hebrews 13:8 HCSB

Our world is in a state of constant change, but God does not change. So, when the world seems to be trembling beneath our feet, we can be comforted in the knowledge that our Heavenly Father is the rock that cannot be shaken. His Word promises, "I am the Lord, I do not change" (Malachi 3:6 NKJV).

Every day that we live, we mortals encounter a multitude of changes—some good, some not so good. And on occasion, all of us must endure life-changing personal losses that leave us breathless. When we do, our loving Heavenly Father stands ready to protect us, to comfort us, to guide us, and, in time, to heal us.

Are you facing difficult circumstances that have left you questioning God's plan for your life? If so, please remember that God is far bigger than any problem you may face. So, instead of worrying about life's inevitable challenges, put your faith in the Father and His only begotten Son: "Jesus Christ is the same yesterday, today, and forever" (Hebrews 13:8 NKJV). Then, rest assured: It is precisely because your Savior does not change that you can face your challenges with courage for today and hope for tomorrow.

But I'm convinced the best way to cope
with change, ironically enough, is to get to
know a God who doesn't change,
One who provides an anchor in
the swirling seas of change.

Bill Hybels

Lord, when we are wrong, make us willing
to change; and when we are right,
make us easy to live with.

Peter Marshall

When you're through changing, you're through!

John Maxwell

Conditions are always changing; therefore,
I must not be dependent upon conditions.
What matters supremely is my soul
and my relationship to God.

Corrie ten Boom

There is a time for everything,
and a season for every activity under heaven.

Ecclesiastes 3:1 NIV

—A PRAYER—

Dear Lord, our world changes,
but You are unchanging. When I face
challenges that leave me discouraged or fearful,
I will turn to You for strength and assurance.
Let my trust in You—like Your love for me—
be unchanging and everlasting.
—Amen—

ADDITIONAL VERSES TO CONSIDER

Proverbs 27:12; Matthew 6:34; James 1:17;
Malachi 3:6; Matthew 18:3, 4

THE POWER OF FAITH

*So then faith comes by hearing,
and hearing by the word of God.*

Romans 10:17 *NKJV*

J esus taught his disciples that if they had faith, they could move mountains. You can too. When you place your faith, your trust, indeed your life it the hands of Christ Jesus, you'll be amazed at the marvelous things He can do. So strengthen your faith through praise, through worship, through Bible study, and through prayer. And trust God's plans. With Him, all things are possible, and He stands ready to open a world of possibilities to you . . . if you have faith.

Concentration camp survivor Corrie ten Boom relied on faith during her long months of imprisonment and torture. Later, despite the fact that four of her family members had died in Nazi death camps, Corrie's faith was unshaken. She wrote, "There is no pit so deep that God's love is not deeper still." Christians take note: Genuine faith in God means faith in all circumstances, happy or sad, joyful or tragic.

If your faith is being tested to the point of breaking, remember that Your Savior is near. If you reach out to Him in faith, He will give you peace and heal your broken spirit. Reach out today. If you touch even the smallest fragment of the Master's garment, He will make you whole.

God cannot believe for us. Faith is a gift of God,
but whether or not we shall act upon that faith
lies altogether within our own power.
We may or we may not, as we choose.

A. W. Tozer

Faith expects from God what is beyond
all expectation.

Andrew Murray

It is faith that saves us, not works,
but the faith that saves us always
produces works.

C. H. Spurgeon

Only God can move mountains,
but faith and prayer can move God.

E. M. Bounds

*The fundamental fact of existence is that this trust
in God, this faith, is the firm foundation
under everything that makes life worth living.*

Hebrews 11:1 MSG

—A Prayer—

Dear Lord, make me Your obedient,
faithful servant. You are with me always.
Give me faith and let me remember that
with Your love and Your power, I can live
courageously and faithfully today
and every day.

—Amen—

Additional verses to consider

2 Chronicles 20:20; 1 Timothy 6:12;
2 Corinthians 5:7; Habakkuk 2:4;
James 2:20

PURPOSEFUL
WORSHIP

*A time is coming and has now come when
the true worshipers will worship the Father in spirit
and truth, for they are the kind of worshipers
the Father seeks. God is spirit, and his worshipers
must worship in spirit and in truth.*

John 4:23, 24 NIV

All of mankind is engaged in worship . . . of one kind or another. The question is not *whether* we worship, but *what* we worship. Some of us choose to worship God. The result is a plentiful harvest of joy, peace, and abundance. Others distance themselves from God by foolishly worshiping things of this earth such as fame, fortune, or personal gratification. To do so is a terrible mistake with eternal consequences.

Whenever we place our love for material possessions above our love for God—or when we yield to the countless temptations of this world—we find ourselves engaged in a struggle between good and evil, a clash between God and Satan. Our responses to these struggles have implications that echo throughout our families and throughout our communities.

How can we ensure that we cast our lot with God? We do so, in part, by the practice of regular worship in the company of fellow believers. When we worship God faithfully and fervently, we are blessed. When we fail to worship God, for whatever reason, we forfeit the spiritual gifts that He intends for us. Every day provides opportunities to put God where He belongs:

at the center of our lives. When we do so, we worship not just with our words, but also with deeds, and that's as it should be. For believers, God comes first. Always first.

Worship is not taught from the pulpit.
It must be learned in the heart.

Jim Elliot

It's our privilege to not only raise our hands in worship but also to combine the visible with the invisible in a rising stream of praise and adoration sent directly to our Father.

Shirley Dobson

Worship and worry cannot live in the same heart; they are mutually exclusive.

Ruth Bell Graham

The fact that we were created to enjoy God and to worship him forever is etched upon our souls.

Jim Cymbala

*Worship the Lord your God and . . .
serve Him only.*

Matthew 4:10 HCSB

—A PRAYER—

Heavenly Father, let today and every day be
a time of worship. Let me worship You,
not only with words and deeds, but also with
my heart. In the quiet moments of the day,
let me praise You and thank You for creating
me, loving me, guiding me, and saving me.
—Amen—

ADDITIONAL VERSES TO CONSIDER

*Matthew 6:33; Psalm 100; Psalm 66:4;
Philippians 2:9-11*

PURPOSE
THROUGH
ENCOURAGEMENT

*Let's see how inventive we can be in encouraging
love and helping out, not avoiding worshipping
together as some do but spurring each other on.*
Hebrews 10:24, 25 MSG

One of the reasons that God placed you here on earth is so that you might become a beacon of encouragement to the world. As a faithful follower of the One from Galilee, you have every reason to be hopeful, and you have every reason to share your hopes with others. When you do, you will discover that hope, like other human emotions, is contagious.

In his letter to the Ephesians, Paul writes, "Do not let any unwholesome talk come out of your mouths, but only what is helpful for building others up according to their needs, that it may benefit those who listen" (v. 29 NIV). This passage reminds us that, as Christians, we are instructed to choose our words carefully so as to build others up through wholesome, honest encouragement. How can we build others up? By celebrating their victories and their accomplishments. As the old saying goes, "When someone does something good, applaud—you'll make two people happy."

Today, look for the good in others and celebrate the good that you find. When you do, you'll be a powerful force of encouragement to your friends and family . . . and a worthy servant to your God.

Discouraged people don't need critics.
They hurt enough already. They don't need
more guilt or piled-on distress.
They need encouragement. They need a refuge,
a willing, caring, available someone.

Charles Swindoll

God is still in the process of dispensing gifts,
and He uses ordinary individuals like us
to develop those gifts in other people.

Howard Hendricks

Words. Do you fully understand their power?
Can any of us really grasp the mighty force
behind the things we say? Do we stop and
think before we speak, considering
the potency of the words we utter?

Joni Eareckson Tada

Patience and encouragement come from God.
And I pray that God will help you all agree
with each other the way Christ Jesus wants.

Romans 15:5 NCV

—A Prayer—

Dear Heavenly Father, because I am Your child,
I am blessed. You have loved me eternally,
cared for me faithfully, and saved me through
the gift of Your Son Jesus. Just as You have lifted
me up, Lord, let me lift up others in a spirit of
encouragement and optimism and hope. And,
if I can help a fellow traveler, even in
a small way, Dear Lord, may the glory be Yours.

—Amen—

ADDITIONAL VERSES TO CONSIDER

Romans 14:19; Proverbs 25:11; Hebrews 3:13;
Ephesians 4:29

TRUSTING GOD'S PLANS

"For I know the plans I have for you,"
declares the Lord, "plans to prosper you and
not to harm you, plans to give you hope and
a future. Then you will call upon me and come and
pray to me, and I will listen to you."

Jeremiah 29:11, 12 NIV

D oes God have a plan for your life? Of course He does! He is trying to lead you along a path of His choosing . . . but He won't force you to follow. God has given you free will, the opportunity to make decisions for yourself: the choice to obey God's Word and to seek His will is yours and yours alone.

When you make the decision to seek God's will for your life—and you should—then you will contemplate His Word, and you will be watchful for His signs. You will associate with fellow believers who will encourage your spiritual growth. And, you will listen to that inner voice that speaks to you in the quiet moments of your daily devotionals.

God intends to use you in wonderful, unexpected ways if you let Him. But be forewarned: the decision to seek God's plan and fulfill His purpose is ultimately a decision that you must make by yourself and for yourself. The consequences of that decision have implications that are both profound and eternal, so choose carefully. And then, as you go about your daily activities, keep your eyes and ears open, as well as your heart, because God is patiently trying to get His message through . . . and there's no better moment than this one for you to help Him.

Seeing that a Pilot steers the ship in which
we sail, who will never allow us to perish even
in the midst of shipwrecks, there is no reason
why our minds should be overwhelmed
with fear and overcome with weariness.

John Calvin

God's grand strategy, birthed in his grace toward
us in Christ, and nurtured through
the obedience of disciplined faith, is to release
us into the redeemed life of our heart,
knowing it will lead us back to him even as
the North Star guides a ship across the vast
unknown surface of the ocean.

John Eldredge

God isn't a talent scout looking for someone
who is "good enough" or "strong enough."
He is looking for someone with a heart
set on Him, and He will do the rest.

Vance Havner

Blessed is he that trusts in the Lord.

Proverbs 16:20 NIV

—A Prayer—

Dear Lord, let me choose Your plans.
You created me, and You have called me to do
Your work here on earth. Today, I choose to
seek Your will and to live it, knowing that
when I trust in You, I am eternally blessed.
—Amen—

Additional verses to consider

*Proverbs 16:9; Philippians 2:13;
Lamentations 3:25, 26; Psalm 127:1;
Psalm 37:23*

GOD'S PURPOSE, GOD'S PEACE

*Live peaceful and quiet lives in
all godliness and holiness.*

1 Timothy 2:2 NIV

Have you found the genuine peace that can be yours through a passionate commitment to Jesus Christ? Or are you still rushing after the illusion of "peace and happiness" that the world promises but cannot deliver? The beautiful words of John 14:27 remind us that Jesus offers us peace, not as the world gives, but as He alone gives: "Peace I leave with you. My peace I give to you. I do not give to you as the world gives. Your heart must not be troubled or fearful" (HCSB). Our challenge is to accept Christ's peace into our hearts and then, as best we can, to share His peace with our neighbors.

Are you at peace with the direction of your life? If you're a Christian, you should be. Perhaps you seek a new direction or a sense of renewed purpose, but those feelings should never rob you of the genuine peace that can and should be yours through a personal relationship with Jesus. The demands of everyday living should never obscure the fact that Christ died so that you might have life abundant and eternal.

Today, as a gift to yourself, to your family, and to your friends, claim the inner peace that is your spiritual birthright: the peace of Jesus Christ. It is offered freely; it has been paid for in full; it is yours for the asking. So ask. And then share.

Prayer guards hearts and minds and causes God to bring peace out of chaos.

Beth Moore

To know God as He really is—in His essential nature and character—is to arrive at a citadel of peace that circumstances may storm, but can never capture.

Catherine Marshall

There may be no trumpet sound or loud applause when we make a right decision, just a calm sense of resolution and peace.

Gloria Gaither

Peace with God is where all peace begins.

Jim Gallery

And let the peace of the Messiah,
to which you were also called in one body,
control your hearts. Be thankful.

Colossians 3:15 HCSB

—A Prayer—

Dear Lord, the peace that the world offers is fleeting, but You offer a peace that is perfect and eternal. Let me take my concerns and burdens to You, Father, and let me feel the spiritual abundance that You offer through the person of Your Son, the Prince of Peace.

—Amen—

Additional verses to consider

1 Corinthians 7:15; Ephesians 2:13, 14;
Haggai 2:6-9; James 3:18; John 14:27

THE COURAGE TO TRUST AND THE COURAGE TO ACT

Behold, God is my salvation;
I will trust, and not be afraid....

Isaiah 12:2 KJV

Every human life is a tapestry of events: some grand, some not-so-grand, and some downright tragic. When we reach the mountaintops of life, praising God is easy. In the moment of triumph, we trust God's plan. But, when the storm clouds form overhead and we find ourselves in the dark valley of despair, our faith is stretched, sometimes to the breaking point. As Christians, we can be comforted: Wherever we find ourselves, whether at the top of the mountain or the depths of the valley, God is there, and because He cares for us, we can live courageously.

Believing Christians have every reason to be courageous. After all, the ultimate battle has already been fought and won on the cross at Calvary. But, even dedicated followers of Christ may find their courage tested by the inevitable disappointments and tragedies that occur in the lives of believers and non-believers alike.

The next time you find your courage tested to the limit, remember that God is as near as your next breath, and remember that He offers salvation to His children. He is your shield and your strength; He is your protector and your deliverer. Call upon Him in your hour of need and then be comforted. Whatever your challenge, whatever your trouble, God can handle it. And will.

What is courage? It is the ability to be strong in trust, in conviction, in obedience.
To be courageous is to step out in faith—
to trust and obey, no matter what.

Kay Arthur

There comes a time when we simply have to face the challenges in our lives and stop backing down.

John Eldredge

Just as courage is faith in good, so discouragement is faith in evil, and, while courage opens the door to good, discouragement opens it to evil.

Hannah Whitall Smith

Therefore, being always of good courage . . .
we walk by faith, not by sight.

2 Corinthians 5:6, 7 NASB

—A Prayer—

Lord, let me turn to You for courage and for strength. When I am fearful, keep me mindful of Your promises. When I am anxious, let me turn my thoughts and prayers to the priceless gift of Your Son. You are with me always, Heavenly Father, and I will face the challenges of this day with trust and assurance in You.

—Amen—

Additional Verses to Consider

1 Chronicles 28:20; 1 Corinthians 16:13;
2 Timothy 1:7; Isaiah 41:10; Joshua 1:9

A Journey
of Spiritual
Growth

Long for the pure milk of the word,
so that by it you may grow in respect to salvation.

1 Peter 2:2 NASB

The journey toward spiritual maturity lasts a lifetime: As Christians, we can and should continue to grow in the love and the knowledge of our Savior as long as we live. When we cease to grow, either emotionally or spiritually, we do ourselves and our loved ones a profound disservice. But, if we study God's Word, if we obey His commandments, and if we live in the center of His will, we will not be "stagnant" believers; we will, instead, be growing Christians . . . and that's exactly what God wants for our lives.

Many of life's most important lessons are painful to learn. During times of heartbreak and hardship, God stands ready to protect us. As Psalm 147 promises, "He heals the brokenhearted and bandages their wounds" (NCV). In His own time and according to His master plan, God will heal us if we invite Him into our hearts.

Spiritual growth need not take place only in times of adversity. We must seek to grow in our knowledge and love of the Lord every day that we live. In those quiet moments when we open our hearts to God, the One who made us keeps remaking us. He gives us direction, perspective, wisdom, and courage. The appropriate moment to accept those spiritual gifts is the present one.

In the midst of the pressure and the heat,
I am confident His hand is on my life,
developing my faith until I display His glory,
transforming me into a vessel of honor that
pleases Him!

Anne Graham Lotz

Some people have received Christ but have
never reached spiritual maturity. We should
grow as Christians every day, and we are not
completely mature until we live in
the presence of Christ.

Billy Graham

Our vision is so limited we can hardly imagine
a love that does not show itself in protection
from suffering. The love of God did not protect
His own Son. He will not necessarily protect
us—not from anything it takes to make us like
His Son. A lot of hammering and chiseling and
purifying by fire will have to go into the process.

Elisabeth Elliot

*For this reason we also, since the day we heard it,
do not cease to pray for you, and to ask that
you may be filled with the knowledge of His will in
all wisdom and spiritual understanding.*

Colossians 1:9 NKJV

—A PRAYER—

Lord, help me to keep growing spiritually
and emotionally. Let me live according
to Your Word, and let me grow in
my faith every day that I live.
—Amen—

ADDITIONAL VERSES TO CONSIDER

*Luke 6:47, 48; Ephesians 3:18, 19; 2 Peter 3:18;
Psalm 66:10-12; Matthew 6:19-21*

THE POWER OF PERSEVERANCE

Let us not become weary in doing good,
for at the proper time we will reap
a harvest if we do not give up.

Galatians 6:9 NIV

As you continue to seek God's purpose for your life, you will undoubtedly experience your fair share of disappointments, detours, false starts, and failures. When you do, don't become discouraged: God's not finished with you yet.

The old saying is as true today as it was when it was first spoken: "Life is a marathon, not a sprint." That's why wise travelers select a traveling companion who never tires and never falters. That partner, of course, is your Heavenly Father.

Are you tired? Ask God for strength. Are you discouraged? Believe in His promises. Are you defeated? Pray as if everything depended upon God, and work as if everything depended upon you.

Perhaps you are in a hurry for God to reveal His plans for your life. If so, be forewarned: God operates on His own timetable, not yours. Sometimes, God may answer your prayers with silence, and when He does, you must patiently persevere. In times of trouble, you must remain steadfast and trust in the merciful goodness of your Heavenly Father. Whatever your problem, He can handle it. Your job is to keep persevering until He does.

By perseverance, the snail reached the ark.

C. H. Spurgeon

Only the man who follows the command of
Jesus single-mindedly and unresistingly lets
his yoke rest upon him, finds his burden easy,
and under its gentle pressure receives
the power to persevere in the right way.

Dietrich Bonhoeffer

That is the source of Jeremiah's living
persistence, his creative constancy. He was
up before the sun, listening to God's word.
Rising early, he was quiet and attentive before
his Lord. Long before the yelling started, the
mocking, the complaining, there was
this centering, discovering, exploring time
with God.

Eugene Peterson

All rising to a great place is by a winding stair.

Francis Bacon

For you have need of endurance,
so that after you have done the will of God,
you may receive the promise.

Hebrews 10:36 NKJV

—A Prayer—

Heavenly Father, sometimes, this life is difficult
indeed. But even in my darkest moments,
You never leave my side. Today, Lord,
let me be a finisher of my faith. Let me
persevere—even if the day is difficult—
and let me follow Your Son Jesus
this day and forever.
—Amen—

Additional verses to consider

Hebrews 12:1; Isaiah 40:3; James 1:12;
James 5:10, 11; Matthew 7:13, 14

GREATNESS THROUGH SERVICE

*So prepare your minds for service
and have self-control.*

1 Peter 1:13 NCV

The teachings of Jesus are clear: We achieve greatness through humble service. So, as you seek to discover God's purpose for your life, you may rest assured that His plan for you is centered around service to your family, to your friends, to your church, to your community, and to the world.

Today, you may feel the temptation to build yourself up in the eyes of your neighbors. Resist that temptation. Instead, serve your neighbors quietly and without fanfare. Find a need and fill it . . . humbly. Lend a helping hand and share a word of kindness . . . anonymously, for this is God's way.

As a humble servant, you will glorify yourself not before men, but before God, and that's what God intends. After all, earthly glory is fleeting: here today and soon gone. But, heavenly glory endures throughout eternity. So the choice is yours: Either you can lift yourself up here on earth and be humbled in heaven, or vice versa. Choose vice versa.

That's what I love about serving God.
In His eyes, there are no little people . . .
because there are no big people.
We are all on the same playing field.

Joni Eareckson Tada

God will open up places of service for you as
He sees you are ready. Meanwhile, study
the Bible and give yourself a chance to grow.

Warren Wiersbe

If you aren't serving, you're just existing,
because life is meant for ministry.

Rick Warren

A Christian is a perfectly free lord of all,
subject to none. A Christian is a perfectly
dutiful servant of all, subject to all.

Martin Luther

Therefore, since we receive a kingdom
which cannot be shaken, let us show gratitude,
by which we may offer to God an acceptable service
with reverence and awe....

Hebrews 12:28 NASB

—A PRAYER—

Dear Lord, in weak moments, I seek to build
myself up by placing myself ahead of others.
But Your commandment, Father, is that
I become a humble servant to those who need
my encouragement, my help, and my love.
Create in me a servant's heart. And, let me
follow in the footsteps of Your Son Jesus who
taught us by example that to be great in
Your eyes, Lord, is to serve others humbly,
faithfully, and lovingly.

—Amen—

ADDITIONAL VERSES TO CONSIDER

John 12:26; Mark 9:35; Matthew 20:26-28;
Matthew 25:37-40; Philippians 2:5-8

BEYOND BUSYNESS

I find rest in God; only he can save me.

Psalm 62:1 NCV

H as the busy pace of life robbed you of the passion and the peace that might otherwise be yours through Jesus Christ? If so, you are simply too busy for your own good. Through His Son Jesus, God offers you a peace that passes human understanding, but He won't force His peace upon you; in order to experience it, you must slow down long enough to sense His presence and His love.

Time is a nonrenewable gift from God. How will you use it? You know from experience that you should invest some time each day in yourself, but finding time to do so is easier said than done. Sometimes, you may have difficulty investing large blocks of time in much-needed thought and self-reflection. If so, it may be time to reorder your priorities.

God has big plans for you. Discovering those plans will require trial and error, meditation and prayer, faith and perseverance. The moments of silence that you claim for yourself will help you gather your thoughts and sense direction from your Creator. And the time that you spend discussing your dreams with friends and mentors can be invaluable. But, no one can force you to carve out time for life's meaningful moments; it's up to you.

Each waking moment holds the potential to think a creative thought or offer a heartfelt prayer. So even if you're a woman with too many demands and too few hours in which to meet them, don't panic. Instead, be comforted in the knowledge that when you sincerely seek to discover God's purpose for your life, He will respond in marvelous and surprising ways. Remember: this is the day that He has made and that He has filled it with countless opportunities to love, to serve, and to seek His guidance. Seize those opportunities today, and keep seizing them every day that you live.

Noise and words and frenzied, hectic schedules dull our senses, closing our ears to His still, small voice and making us numb to His touch.

Charles Swindoll

We often become mentally and spiritually barren because we're so busy.

Franklin Graham

In quietness and trust is your strength.

Isaiah 30:15 NASB

—A Prayer—

Dear Lord, when the quickening pace of life leaves me with little time for worship or for praise, help me to reorder my priorities. When the demands of the day leave me distracted and discouraged, let me turn to Jesus for the peace that only He can give. And then, when I have accepted the spiritual abundance that is mine through Christ, let me share His message and His love with all who cross my path.

—Amen—

Additional Verses to Consider

Psalm 46:10; Isaiah 50:4, 5; Luke 5:16

DISCOVERING THE POWER OF OPTIMISM

*For God has not given us a spirit of fearfulness,
but one of power, love, and sound judgment.*

2 Timothy 1:7 HCSB

Are you an optimistic, passionate, enthusiastic Christian? You should be. After all, as a believer, you have every reason to be optimistic about life here on earth *and* life eternal. As C. H. Spurgeon observed, "Our hope in Christ for the future is the mainstream of our joy." But sometimes, you may find yourself pulled down by the inevitable demands and worries of life here on earth. If you find yourself discouraged, exhausted, or both, then it's time to take your concerns to God. When you do, He will lift your spirits and renew your strength.

Are you willing to trust God's plans for your life? Hopefully, you will trust Him completely. Proverbs 3:5, 6 makes it clear: "Trust in the Lord with all your heart, and lean not on your own understanding; in all your ways acknowledge Him, and He shall direct your paths" (NKJV).

Today, make this promise to yourself and keep it: vow to be a hope-filled Christian. Think optimistically about your life, your profession, your family, your future, and your purpose for living. Trust your hopes, not your fears. Take time to celebrate God's glorious creation. And then, when you've filled your heart with hope

and gladness, share your optimism with others.
They'll be better for it, and so will you.

If you can't tell whether your glass is half-empty
of half-full, you don't need another glass;
what you need is better eyesight . . .
and a more thankful heart.

Marie T. Freeman

The popular idea of faith is of a certain
obstinate optimism: the hope, tenaciously
held in the face of trouble,
that the universe is fundamentally friendly
and things may get better.

J. I. Packer

Christ can put a spring in your step and
a thrill in your heart. Optimism and
cheerfulness are products of knowing Christ.

Billy Graham

I can do everything through him
that gives me strength.

Philippians 4:13 NIV

—A Prayer—

Lord, give me faith, optimism, and hope.
Let me expect the best from You, and let me
look for the best in others. Let me trust You,
Lord, to direct my life. And, let me be
Your faithful, hopeful, optimistic servant
every day that I live.
—Amen—

Additional verses to consider

Psalm 23:5, 6; Romans 8:25; Psalm 51:8;
Psalm 31:24; Psalm 27:1

Choices That Are Pleasing to God

So we make it our goal to please him....

2 Corinthians 5:9 NIV

I f you're like most people, you seek the admiration of your neighbors, your coworkers, and, most importantly, your family members. But the eagerness to please others should never overshadow your eagerness to please God. If you seek to fulfill the purposes that God has in store for you, then you must seek to please Him first and always.

Each new day presents countless opportunities to put God in first place . . . or not. When we honor God by making choices that are pleasing to Him, we earn for ourselves the abundance and peace that He promises. But, when we concern ourselves more with pleasing others than with pleasing our Creator, we bring needless suffering upon ourselves and our families.

Would you like a time-tested formula for successful living? Here is a formula that is proven and true: Seek God's approval in every aspect of your life. Does this sound too simple? Perhaps it is simple, but it is also the only way to reap the marvelous riches that God has in store for You.

Make God's will the focus of your life day by
day. If you seek to please Him and Him alone,
you'll find yourself satisfied with life.

Kay Arthur

Get ready for God to show you not only
His pleasure, but His approval.

Joni Eareckson Tada

All our offerings, whether music or martyrdom,
are like the intrinsically worthless present of
a child, which a father values indeed,
but values only for the intention.

C. S. Lewis

You will get untold flak for prioritizing God's
revealed and present will for your life
over man's . . . but, boy, is it worth it.

Beth Moore

Do you think I am trying to make people accept me?
No, God is the One I am trying to please.
Am I trying to please people? If I still wanted to
please people, I would not be a servant of Christ.

Galatians 1:10 NCV

—A PRAYER—

Dear Lord, today I will honor You with my
thoughts, my actions, and my prayers.
I will seek to please You, and I will strive to
serve You. Your blessings are as limitless as
Your love. And because I have been so
richly blessed, I will worship You, Father,
with thanksgiving in my heart and praise
on my lips, this day and forever.

—Amen—

ADDITIONAL VERSES TO CONSIDER

1 Corinthians 4:3, 4; 1 Timothy 2:3, 4;
Hebrews 1:6; Colossians 1:10; 1 Peter 2:19

BEYOND OUR DISAPPOINTMENTS AND FAILURES

I have heard your prayer, I have seen your tears;
behold, I will heal you....

2 Kings 20:5 RSV

From time to time, all of us face life-altering disappointments that leave us breathless. Oftentimes, these disappointments come unexpectedly, leaving us with more questions than answers. But even when we don't have all the answers—or, for that matter, even when we don't seem to have any of the answers—God does.

If your faith is being tested by difficult circumstances, perhaps it's time to ask yourself three important questions:

1. How does God want me to respond?

2. What does God want me to learn?

3. Where does God want me to go from here?

Hidden within every disappointment is the potential for personal and spiritual growth. Life's darker days are filled with "teachable moments"—moments that offer unique learning opportunities. During these moments, God has things that He wants to say specifically to you. You, in turn, must make yourself open to His instructions.

Your Heavenly Father has a perfect plan and a chosen path for all of His children, including you. When tough times arrive, you should learn from your experiences and you should prayerfully seek God's guidance for the future. Then, you should get busy with the work at hand—the difficult and rewarding work of overcoming your disappointments. When you do your part, you can be certain that God will do His part. And you can be sure that in time, your loving Heavenly Father will turn your stumbling blocks into stepping stones.

What may seem defeat to us may
be victory to him.

C. H. Spurgeon

If your hopes are being disappointed just now,
it means that they are being purified.

Oswald Chambers

The next time you're disappointed, don't panic.
Don't give up. Just be patient and let God
remind you he's still in control.

Max Lucado

*For we do not want you to be ignorant, brethren,
of our trouble which came to us in Asia: that we
were burdened beyond measure, above strength,
so that we despaired even of life. Yes, we had
the sentence of death in ourselves, that we should
not trust in ourselves but in God who raises
the dead, who delivered us from so great a death,
and does deliver us; in whom we trust that
He will still deliver us.*

2 Corinthians 1:8-10 NKJV

—A PRAYER—

Dear Lord, when I am disappointed,
give me perspective and faith. When I am weak,
give me strength. When I am fearful,
give me courage for the day ahead. I will trust in
Your promises, Father, and I will live with
the assurance that You are with me not only for
this day, but also throughout all eternity.

—Amen—

ADDITIONAL VERSES TO CONSIDER

*Psalm 18:28; Proverbs 17:22; Proverbs 12:25;
Joshua 1:9; 1 Chronicles 28:20*

PURPOSE AND TRANSFORMATION

*And do not be conformed to this world,
but be transformed by the renewing of your mind,
so that you may prove what the will of God is,
that which is good and acceptable and perfect.*

Romans 12:2 NASB

God has the power to transform your life if you invite Him to do so. Your decision is straightforward: whether or not to allow the Father's transforming power to work in you and through you. God stands at the door and waits; all you must do is knock. When you do, God always answers.

Sometimes, the demands of daily life may drain you of strength or rob you of the joy that is rightfully yours in Christ. But even on your darkest day, you may be comforted by the knowledge that God has the power to renew your spirit and your life.

Are you in need of a new beginning? If so, turn your heart toward God in prayer. Are you weak or worried? Take the time—or, more accurately, make the time—to delve deeply into God's Holy Word. Are you spiritually depleted? Call upon fellow believers to support you, and call upon Christ to renew your sense of joy and thanksgiving. When you do, you'll discover that the Creator of the universe is in the business of making all things new—including you.

In the midst of the pressure and the heat,
I am confident His hand is on my life,
developing my faith until I display His glory,
transforming me into a vessel of honor
that pleases Him!

Anne Graham Lotz

God's work is not in buildings,
but in transformed lives.

Ruth Bell Graham

God became man to turn creatures into sons:
not simply to produce better men of
the old kind but to produce a new kind of man.

C. S. Lewis

God has sent His Holy Spirit to transform us
into more accurate reflections of who God is....

Bill Hybels

And He who sits on the throne said,
"Behold, I am making all things new."

Revelation 21:5 NASB

—A Prayer—

Dear Lord, You have the power to make
all things new. When I grow weary, let me
turn my thoughts and my prayers to You. When
I am discouraged, restore my faith in You.
Renew my strength, Father, and let me draw
comfort and courage from Your promises
and from Your unending love.

—Amen—

Additional Verses to Consider

2 Corinthians 5:17; Isaiah 43:18, 19;
Matthew 11:28–30; Proverbs 24:16;
Psalm 23:2, 3

ASKING GOD

You do not have, because you do not ask God.

James 4:2 NIV

Have you fervently asked God to help you discover His purpose for Your life? Have you asked Him for guidance and for strength? If so, then you're continually inviting your Creator to reveal Himself in a variety of ways. As a follower of Christ, you must do no less.

Jesus made it clear to His disciples: they should petition God to meet their needs. So should we. Genuine, heartfelt prayer produces powerful changes in us and in our world. When we lift our hearts to God, we open ourselves to a never-ending source of divine wisdom and infinite love.

Do you have questions about your future that you simply can't answer? Do you have needs that you simply can't meet by yourself? Do you sincerely seek to know God's unfolding plans for your life? If so, ask Him for direction, for protection, and for strength—and then keep asking Him every day that you live. Whatever your need, no matter how great or small, pray about it and never lose hope. God is not just near; He is here, and He's perfectly capable of answering your prayers. Now, it's up to you to ask.

We honor God by asking for great things when they are a part of His promise. We dishonor Him and cheat ourselves when we ask for molehills where He has promised mountains.

Vance Havner

We get into trouble when we think we *know* what to do and we stop *asking God* if we're doing it.

Stormie Omartian

God makes prayer as easy as possible for us. He's completely approachable and available, and He'll never mock or upbraid us for bringing our needs before Him.

Shirley Dobson

Notice that we must ask. And we will sometimes struggle to hear and struggle with what we hear. But personally, it's worth it. I'm after the path of life— and he alone knows it.

John Eldredge

*So I say to you, keep asking, and it will be given
to you. Keep searching, and you will find.
Keep knocking, and the door will be opened to you.*
Luke 11:9 HCSB

—A Prayer—

Dear Lord, today I will ask You for the things
I need. In every circumstance, in every season
of life, I will come to you in prayer. You know
the desires of my heart, Lord; grant them, I ask.
Yet not my will, Father, but Your will be done.
—Amen—

Additional verses to consider

*John 14:12-14; John 15:16; Matthew 7:7, 8
Philippians 4:6; John 16:23, 24*

OUR WEAKNESSES AND GOD'S STRENGTH

The Lord is my light and my salvation;
whom shall I fear? The Lord is the strength
of my life; of whom shall I be afraid?

Psalms 27:1 NKJV

God is a never-ending source of strength and courage when we call upon Him. When we are weary, He gives us strength. When we see no hope, God reminds us of His promises. When we grieve, God wipes away our tears.

Do you feel burdened by today's responsibilities? Do you feel pressured by the ever-increasing demands of 21st-century life? Then turn your concerns and your prayers over to God. He knows your needs, and He has promised to meet those needs. Whatever your circumstances, God will protect you and care for you if you allow Him to preside over your life. So today and every day, be passionate in your determination to allow God to rule over your mind and your heart.

Life can be challenging, but fear not. God loves you, and He will protect you. Whatever your challenge, God can handle it. Let Him.

Measure the size of the obstacles against
the size of God.

Beth Moore

God walks with us. He scoops us up in His arms
or simply sits with us in silent strength until we
cannot avoid the awesome recognition that yes,
even now, He is here.

Gloria Gaither

And in truth, if we only knew it, our chief
fitness is our utter helplessness. His strength is
made perfect, not in our strength, but in our
weakness. Our strength is only a hindrance.

Hannah Whitall Smith

Our Lord never drew power from Himself,
He drew it always from His Father.

Oswald Chambers

The LORD is my strength and my song . . . .

Exodus 15:2 NIV

—A PRAYER—

Dear Lord, let me turn to You for strength.
When I am weak, You lift me up.
When my spirit is crushed, You comfort me.
When I am victorious, Your Word reminds me
to be humble. Today and every day,
I will turn to You, Father, for strength, for hope,
for wisdom, and for salvation.
—Amen—

ADDITIONAL VERSES TO CONSIDER

1 Chronicles 28:20; Matthew 11:28-30;
Proverbs 24:10; Psalm 105:4, 5; Psalm 46:1

A JOURNEY OF PRAYER AND MEDITATION

The intense prayer of the righteous is very powerful.

James 5:16 HCSB

Once you finally discover God's purpose for your life, you search will be over and your life will be complete . . . right? Wrong! Your search to discover God's unfolding plan for your life is not a destination to be reached; it is a path to be traveled, a journey that unfolds day by day. And, that's exactly how often you should seek direction from your Creator: one day at a time, each day followed by the next, without exception.

Daily prayer and meditation is a matter of will and habit. You must willingly organize your time by carving out quiet moments with God, and you must form the habit of daily worship. When you do, you'll discover that no time is more precious than the silent moments you spend with your Heavenly Father.

God promises that the prayers of righteous people can accomplish great things. God promises that He answers prayer (although His answers are not always in accordance with our desires). God invites us to be still and to feel His presence. So pray. Pray about matters great and small; and be watchful for the answers that God most assuredly sends your way.

The remedy for distractions is the same now as
it was in earlier and simpler times:
prayer, meditation, and the cultivation
of the inner life.

A. W. Tozer

I need the spiritual revival that comes from
spending quiet time alone with Jesus in prayer
and in thoughtful meditation on His Word.

Anne Graham Lotz

Speed-reading may be a good thing,
but it was never meant for the Bible. It takes
calm, thoughtful, prayerful meditation on
the Word to extract its deepest nourishment.

Vance Havner

Four things let us ever keep in mind:
God hears prayer, God heeds payer,
God answers prayer, and God delivers by prayer.

E. M. Bounds

And when they had prayed, the place was shaken
where they were assembled together;
and they were all filled with the Holy Ghost,
and they spake the word of God with boldness.

Acts 4:31 KJV

—A Prayer—

Dear Lord, make me a person whose constant
prayers are pleasing to You. Let me come to
You often with concerns both great and small.
I trust in the power of prayer, Father, because
prayer changes things and it changes me.
In the quiet moments of the day, I will open
my heart to You. I know that You are with me
always and that You always hear my prayers.
So I will pray and be thankful.

—Amen—

Additional verses to consider

Joel 2:32; Luke 18:1; Mark 11:25;
Psalm 19:14; Romans 12:12

PURPOSE THROUGH DISCIPLESHIP

Then said Jesus unto his disciples,
If any man will come after me,
let him deny himself, and take up his cross,
and follow me.

Matthew 16:24 KJV

When we have been saved by Christ, we can, if we choose, become passive Christians. We can sit back, secure in our own salvation, and let other believers spread the healing message of Jesus. But to do so is wrong. Instead, we are commanded to become passionate disciples of the One who has saved us, and to do otherwise is a sin of omission with terrible consequences.

When Jesus addressed His disciples, He warned them that each one must, "take up his cross daily and follow me" (Luke 9:23 NIV). Christ's message was clear: In order to follow Him, Christ's disciples must deny themselves and, instead, trust Him completely. Nothing has changed since then.

If we are to be disciples of Christ, we must trust Him and place Him at very center of our beings. Jesus never comes "next." He is always first. The wonderful paradox, of course, is that it is only by sacrificing ourselves to Him that we gain eternal salvation.

Do you seek to fulfill God's purpose for your life? Then follow Christ. Follow Him by picking up His cross today and every day that you live.

Then, you will quickly discover that Christ's love has the power to change everything, including you.

Christian discipleship is a process of paying more and more attention to God's righteousness and less and less attention to our own; finding the meaning of our lives not by probing our moods and motives and morals, but by believing in God's will and purposes; making a map of the faithfulness of God, not charting the rise and fall of our enthusiasms.

Eugene Peterson

A follower is never greater than his leader; a follower never draws attention to himself.

Franklin Graham

There is not Christianity without a cross, for you cannot be a disciple of Jesus without taking up your cross.

Henry Blackaby

*But the eleven disciples proceeded to Galilee,
to the mountain which Jesus had designated.
When they saw Him, they worshiped Him; but
some were doubtful. And Jesus came up and spoke
to them, saying, "All authority has been given to
Me in heaven and on earth. Go therefore and make
disciples of all the nations, baptizing them in
the name of the Father and the Son and
the Holy Spirit, teaching them to observe all that
I commanded you; and lo, I am with you always,
even to the end of the age."*

Matthew 28:16-20 NASB

—A Prayer—

Dear Lord, thank You for the gift of Your Son
Jesus, my personal savior. Let me be a worthy
disciple of Christ, and let me be ever grateful for
His love. I offer my life to You, Lord, so that I
might live according to Your plan. I will praise
You always as I give thanks for Your Son and for
Your everlasting love.

—Amen—

ADDITIONAL VERSES TO CONSIDER

John 13:34, 35; Luke 9:1, 2; Luke 18:1

ACCEPTING THE PAST AND PLANNING FOR THE FUTURE

One thing I do, forgetting those things which are behind and reaching forward to those things which are ahead, I press toward the goal for the prize of the upward call of God in Christ Jesus.

Philippians 3:13-14 NKJV

Some of life's greatest roadblocks are not the ones we see through the windshield; they are, instead, the roadblocks that seem to fill the rearview mirror. Sometimes, because we are imperfect human beings, we find it difficult to accept the past. We simply can't seem to let go of our pain, so we relive it . . . with predictably unfortunate consequences.

Of course, no amount of anger or bitterness can change what happened yesterday. Tears can't change the past; regrets can't change it. Our worries won't change the past, and neither will our complaints. Simply put, the past is, and always will be, the past. Forever.

Can you summon the courage (and the wisdom) to accept the past and move on with your life? Hopefully you can. Then, you can fully engage yourself in the present and, by doing so, build a better future for yourself and your loved ones.

So, if you've endured a difficult past, accept it and learn from it, but don't spend too much time there. Instead, trust God's plan for your life and look to the future for God's blessings. He intends to use you in wonderful, unexpected ways if you let Him. The decision to seek God's plan and look to the future is an important decision . . . and it's the right thing to do. Don't let bitterness—or any other sin—get in the way.

Shake the dust from your past,
and move forward in His promises.

Kay Arthur

Our yesterdays present irreparable things to us; it is true that we have lost opportunities which will never return, but God can transform this destructive anxiety into a constructive thoughtfulness for the future. Let the past sleep, but let it sleep on the bosom of Christ. Leave the Irreparable Past in His hands, and step out into the Irresistible Future with Him.

Oswald Chambers

The pages of your past cannot be rewritten, but the pages of your tomorrows are blank.

Zig Ziglar

We can't just put our pasts behind us.
We've got to put our pasts in front of God.

Beth Moore

The Lord says, "Forget what happened before,
and do not think about the past. Look at the new
thing I am going to do. It is already happening.
Don't you see it? I will make a road in
the desert and rivers in the dry land."

Isaiah 43:18-19 NCV

—A PRAYER—

Dear Lord, let me live in the present,
not the past. Let me focus on my blessings,
not my sorrows. Give me the wisdom to be
thankful for the gifts that I do have, not bitter
about the things that I don't have. Let me
accept what was, let me give thanks for what is,
and let me have faith in what most surely will
be: the promise of eternal life with You.

—Amen—

ADDITIONAL VERSES TO CONSIDER

Jeremiah 29:11; Proverbs 24:14; Proverbs 27:1;
Proverbs 21:5; Psalm 20:4

LIVING WITH GOD'S WORD

For the word of God is living and effective and sharper than any two-edged sword, penetrating as far as to divide soul, spirit, joints, and marrow; it is a judge of the ideas and thoughts of the heart.

Hebrews 4:12 HCSB

God's Word is unlike any other book. The Bible is a roadmap for life here on earth and for life eternal. As Christians, we are called upon to study God's Holy Word, to trust His Word, to follow its commandments, and to share its Good News with the world.

The words of Matthew 4:4 remind us that, "Man shall not live by bread alone but by every word that proceedeth out of the mouth of God." (KJV). As believers, we must study the Bible and meditate upon its meaning for our lives. Otherwise, we deprive ourselves of a priceless gift from our Creator.

Warren Wiersbe observed, "When the child of God looks into the Word of God, he sees the Son of God. And, he is transformed by the Spirit of God to share in the glory of God." God's Holy Word is, indeed, a transforming, life-changing, one-of-a-kind treasure. And, a passing acquaintance with the Good Book is insufficient for Christians who seek to obey God's Word and to understand His will. After all, men—and women—do not live by bread alone . . .

God's voice isn't all that difficult to hear.
He sometimes shouts through our pain,
whispers to us while we're relaxing on vacation,
occasionally, He sings to us in a song, and warns
us through the sixty-six books of His written
Word. It's right there, ink on paper. Count on
it—that book will never lead you astray.

Charles Swindoll

God's Word is a light not only to our path but
also to our thinking. Place it in your heart
today, and you will never walk in darkness.

Joni Eareckson Tada

If we are not continually fed with God's Word,
we will starve spiritually.

Stormie Omartian

The Word of God, prayer, and suffering are
the three "tools" that God uses in our lives.

Warren Wiersbe

For as the rain comes down, and the snow from heaven, and do not return there, but water the earth, and make it bring forth and bud, that it may give seed to the sower and bread to the eater, so shall My word be that goes forth from My mouth; it shall not return to Me void, but it shall accomplish what I please, and it shall prosper in the thing for which I sent it.

Isaiah 55:10, 11 NKJV

—A PRAYER—

Heavenly Father, Your Holy Word is a light unto the world; let me study it, trust it, and share it with all who cross my path. In all that I do, help me be a worthy witness for You as I share the Good News of Your perfect Son and Your perfect Word.

—Amen—

ADDITIONAL VERSES TO CONSIDER

1 Peter 1:25; 1 Thessalonians 1:5; 2 Timothy 3:16; Matthew 4:4; Psalm 119:105

FOLLOWING IN HIS FOOTSTEPS

If anyone serves Me, let him follow Me;
and where I am, there My servant will be also.
If anyone serves Me, him My Father will honor.

John 12:26 *NKJV*

Jesus loved you so much that He endured unspeakable humiliation and pain: the "passion" that Luke describes in Acts 1:3. How will you respond to Christ's sacrifice? Will you take up His cross and follow Him (Luke 9: 23) or will you choose another path? When you place your hopes squarely at the foot of the cross, when you place Jesus squarely at the center of your life, you will be blessed.

The old familiar hymn begins, "What a friend we have in Jesus . . . ." No truer words were ever penned. Jesus is the sovereign friend and ultimate savior of mankind. Christ showed enduring love for His believers by willingly sacrificing His own life so that we might have eternal life. Now, it is our turn to become His friend.

It's time to take the next step on your life's journey—make certain that you take that step with Christ by your side. Accept His love, obey His teachings, and share His message with your neighbors and with the world. When you do, you will demonstrate that your acquaintance with the Master is not a passing fancy; it is, instead, the foundation and the cornerstone of your life.

Our responsibility is to feed from Him,
to stay close to Him, to follow Him—because
sheep easily go astray—so that we eternally
experience the protection and companionship
of our Great Shepherd the Lord Jesus Christ.

Franklin Graham

Christ is like a river that is continually flowing.
There are always fresh supplies of water coming
from the fountain-head, so that a man may live
by it and be supplied with water all his life.
So Christ is an ever-flowing fountain;
he is continually supplying his people, and
the fountain is not spent. They who live upon
Christ may have fresh supplies from him for
all eternity; they may have an increase of
blessedness that is new, and new still,
and which never will come to an end.

Jonathan Edwards

A believer comes to Christ;
a disciple follows after Him.

Vance Havner

There is therefore now no condemnation to those who are in Christ Jesus, who do not walk according to the flesh, but according to the Spirit.

Romans 8:1 NKJV

—A Prayer—

Dear Lord, You sent Your Son so that I might have abundant life and eternal life. Thank You, Father, for my Savior, Christ Jesus. I will follow Him, honor Him, and share His Good News, this day and every day.

—Amen—

ADDITIONAL VERSES TO CONSIDER

Matthew 9:9; Luke 9:23, 24; Luke 10:39; John 14:23

PURPOSE FOR TODAY . . . PURPOSE FOR ETERNITY

He has made everything beautiful in its time.
He has also set eternity in the hearts of men;
yet they cannot fathom what God has done
from beginning to end.

Ecclesiastes 3:11 NIV

As mere mortals, our vision for the future, like our lives here on earth, is limited. God's vision is not burdened by such limitations: His plans extend throughout all eternity. Thus, God's plans for you are not limited to the ups and downs of everyday life. Your Heavenly Father has bigger things in mind . . . much bigger things.

Christ sacrificed His life on the cross so that we might have eternal life. This gift, freely given by God's only begotten Son, is the priceless possession of everyone who accepts Him as Lord and Savior.

Let us praise the Creator for His priceless gift, and let us share the Good News with all who cross our paths. We return our Father's love by accepting His grace and by sharing His message and His love. When we do, we are blessed here on earth and throughout all eternity.

As you struggle with the inevitable hardships and occasional disappointments of everyday life, remember that God has invited you to accept His abundance not only for today but also for all eternity. So keep things in perspective. Although you will inevitably encounter occasional defeats in this world, you'll have all eternity to celebrate the ultimate victory in the next.

The unfolding of our friendship with the Father
will be a never-ending revelation stretching
on into eternity.

Catherine Marshall

All that is not eternal is eternally out of date.

C. S. Lewis

The damage done to us on this earth will never
find its way into that safe city. We can relax,
we can rest, and though some of us can hardly
imagine it, we can prepare to feel safe and
secure for all of eternity.

Bill Hybels

As I contemplate all the sacrifices required in
order to live a life that is totally focused on
Jesus Christ and His eternal kingdom,
the joy seeps out of my heart onto my face
in a smile of deep satisfaction.

Anne Graham Lotz

*But grow in the grace and knowledge of our Lord
and Savior Jesus Christ. To Him be the glory,
both now and to the day of eternity.*

2 Peter 3:18 NASB

—A Prayer—

I know, Lord, this world is not my home;
I am only here for a short time. You have given
me the priceless gift of eternal life through
Your Son Jesus. Keep the promise of heaven
in my heart, and help me to pass through this
world with joy, with perspective,
with thanksgiving, and with praise
on my lips for You.
—Amen—

ADDITIONAL VERSES TO CONSIDER

*John 4:13, 14; 1 John 5:13;
1 Corinthians 15:51-57; 1 John 5:11,12;
John 3:16*

MORE BIBLE VERSES TO CONSIDER

JESUS

Jesus Christ is the same yesterday, today,
and forever.

Hebrews 13:8 HCSB

In the beginning was the Word, and the Word
was with God, and the Word was God....
And the Word was made flesh, and dwelt among
us, (and we beheld his glory, the glory as of the only
begotten of the Father,) full of grace and truth.

John 1:1, 14 KJV

The next day John seeth Jesus coming unto him,
and saith, Behold the Lamb of God,
which taketh away the sin of the world.

John 1:29 KJV

Jesus answered them, "I told you, and you do not
believe; the works that I do in My Father's name,
these testify of Me."

John 10:25 NASB

CHRIST'S LOVE

Who shall separate us from the love of Christ?
Shall tribulation, or distress, or persecution, or
famine, or nakedness, or peril, or sword?
Yet in all these things we are more than conquerors
through Him who loved us.

Romans 8:35, 37 NKJV

For I am convinced that neither death, nor life,
nor angels, nor principalities, nor things present,
nor things to come, nor powers, nor height, nor
depth, nor any other created thing, will be able to
separate us from the love of God,
which is in Christ Jesus our Lord.

Romans 8:38, 39 NASB

As the Father loved Me, I also have loved you;
abide in My love.

John 15:9 NKJV

Greater love has no one than this,
than to lay down one's life for his friends.

John 15:13 NKJV

COURAGE

But Moses said to the people, "Do not fear!
Stand by and see the salvation of the LORD."

Exodus 14:13 NASB

I leave you peace; my peace I give you.
I do not give it to you as the world does.
So don't let your hearts be troubled or afraid.

John 14:27 NCV

Be not afraid; only believe.

Mark 5:36 NKJV

So He said, "Come." And when Peter had come
down out of the boat, he walked on the water to
go to Jesus. But when he saw that the wind was
boisterous, he was afraid; and beginning to sink
he cried out, saying, "Lord, save me!"
And immediately Jesus stretched out His hand and
caught him, and said to him, "O you of little faith,
why did you doubt?" And when they got into
the boat, the wind ceased.

Matthew 14:29-32 NKJV

FEAR NOT, FOR I HAVE
REDEEMED YOU;
I HAVE CALLED YOU
BY YOUR NAME;
YOU ARE MINE.
—

Isaiah 43:1 NKJV

PERSEVERANCE

We are hard pressed on every side, yet not crushed;
we are perplexed, but not in despair.

2 Corinthians 4:8 NKJV

I have fought a good fight,
I have finished my course, I have kept the faith.

2 Timothy 4:7 KJV

It is better to finish something than to start it.
It is better to be patient than to be proud.

Ecclesiastes 7:8 NCV

Let us lay aside every weight and the sin that so
easily ensnares us, and run with endurance the race
that lies before us, keeping our eyes on Jesus,
the source and perfecter of our faith.

Hebrews 12:1, 2 HCSB

Those who hope in the LORD will renew their
strength. They will soar on wings like eagles;
they will run and not grow weary,
they will walk and not be faint.

Isaiah 40:31 NIV

HOPE

Let us hold fast the confession of our hope without wavering, for He who promised is faithful.

Hebrews 10:23 NKJV

*The LORD is good to those who wait for Him,
To the person who seeks Him. It is good that he waits silently
For the salvation of the LORD.*

Lamentations 3:25, 26 NASB

Hope deferred makes the heart sick.

Proverbs 13:12 NKJV

*Sustain me according to Your word, that I may live;
And do not let me be ashamed of my hope.*

Psalm 119:116 NASB

*For I hope in You, O LORD;
You will answer, O Lord my God.*

Psalm 38:15 NASB

SERVICE

Whatever you do, work at it with all your heart, as working for the Lord, not for men, since you know that you will receive an inheritance from the Lord as a reward. It is the Lord Christ you are serving.

Colossians 3:23, 24 NIV

Suppose a brother or a sister is without clothes and daily food. If one of you says to him, "Go, I wish you well; keep warm and well fed," but does nothing about his physical needs, what good is it?

James 2:15, 16 NIV

Each of you should look not only to your own interests, but also to the interest of others.

Philippians 2:4 NIV

The one who blesses others is abundantly blessed; those who help others are helped.

Proverbs 11:25 MSG

THE POWER OF FAITH

Therefore we conclude that a man is justified by faith without the deeds of the law.

Romans 3:28 KJV

Blessed is the man whose strength is in You, whose heart is set on pilgrimage.

Psalm 84:5 NKJV

Those who hope in the LORD will inherit the land.

Psalm 37:9 NIV

Blessed are they that put their trust in him.

Psalm 2:12 KJV

ATTITUDE

*Therefore, since Christ suffered in his body,
arm yourselves also with the same attitude,
because he who has suffered in his body is done with
sin. As a result, he does not live the rest of
his earthly life for evil human desires,
but rather for the will of God.*

1 Peter 4:1, 2 NIV

*You were taught, with regard to your former
way of life, to put off your old self, which is being
corrupted by its deceitful desires; to be made new in
the attitude of your minds; and to put on the new
self, created to be like God in true righteousness
and holiness.*

Ephesians 4:22-24 NIV

*Finally brothers, whatever is true, whatever is
honorable, whatever is just, whatever is pure,
whatever is lovely, whatever is commendable—
if there is any moral excellence and
if there is any praise—dwell on these things.*

Philippians 4:8 HCSB

KEEP YOUR EYES FOCUSED ON WHAT IS RIGHT, AND LOOK STRAIGHT AHEAD TO WHAT IS GOOD.

—

Proverbs 4:25 NCV

PRAISE

Enter into His gates with thanksgiving,
and into His courts with praise. Be thankful to
Him, and bless His name. For the Lord is good;
His mercy is everlasting,
and His truth endures to all generations.

Psalm 100:4, 5 NKJV

Through Him then, let us continually offer up
a sacrifice of praise to God, that is,
the fruit of lips that give thanks to His name.

Hebrews 13:15 NASB

The LORD is my strength and song,
and He has become my salvation; He is my God,
and I will praise Him.

Exodus 15:2 NIV

Praise the Lord! Happy are those who respect
the Lord, who want what he commands.

Psalm 112:1 NCV

I WILL PRAISE YOU WITH MY WHOLE HEART.

—

Psalm 138:1 NKJV

POWER

*I pray also that you will have greater understanding
in your heart so you will know the hope to which
he has called us and that you will know how rich
and glorious are the blessings God has promised
his holy people. And you will know that
God's power is very great for us who believe.*

Ephesians 1:18, 19 NCV

*If I speak God's Word with power, revealing
all his mysteries and making everything plain as day,
and if I have faith that says to a mountain, "Jump,"
and it jumps, but I don't love, I'm nothing.*

1 Corinthians 13:2 MSG

*"Bring to the storehouse a full tenth of what you
earn so there will be food in my house. Test me in
this," says the Lord All-Powerful. "I will open the
windows of heaven for you and pour out
all the blessings you need."*

Malachi 3:10 NCV

FOR I AM NOT
ASHAMED OF
THE GOSPEL, BECAUSE
IT IS GOD'S POWER
FOR SALVATION
TO EVERYONE WHO
BELIEVES.

—

Romans 1:16 HCSB

JOY

He will exult over you with joy,
He will be quiet in His love.

Zephaniah 3:17 NASB

And not only so, but we also joy in God through
our Lord Jesus Christ,
by whom we have now received the atonement.

Romans 5:11 KJV

May the God of hope fill you with all joy and
peace as you trust in him, so that you may
overflow with hope by the power of the Holy Spirit.

Romans 15:13 NIV

Light shines on those who do right; joy belongs to
those who are honest. Rejoice in the Lord,
you who do right. Praise his holy name.

Psalm 97:11, 12 NCV

Rejoice in the Lord always. I will say it again:
Rejoice!

Philippians 4:4 HCSB

THANKSGIVING

*O come, let us sing unto the L*ORD*: let us make
a joyful noise to the rock of our salvation.
Let us come before his presence with thanksgiving,
and make a joyful noise unto him with psalms.*

Psalm 95:1, 2 KJV

*All Your works shall give thanks to You, O L*ORD*,
And Your godly ones shall bless You.*

Psalm 145:10 NASB

*Make a joyful noise unto the Lord all ye lands.
Serve the Lord with gladness: come before his
presence with singing. Know ye that the Lord he
is God: it is he that hath made us, and not we
ourselves; we are his people and the sheep of his
pasture. Enter into his gates with thanksgiving,
and into his courts with praise; be thankful unto
him and bless his name. For the Lord is good;
his mercy is everlasting; and his truth endureth
to all generations.*

Psalm 100 KJV

GOD'S WORD

*There's nothing like the written Word of God
for showing you the way to salvation through faith
in Christ Jesus. Every part of Scripture is
God-breathed and useful one way or another,
showing us truth, exposing our rebellion, correcting
our mistakes, training us to live God's way.
Through the Word we are put together and shaped
up for the tasks God has for us.*

2 Timothy 3:15-17 MSG

*Therefore whosoever heareth these sayings of mine,
and doeth them, I will liken him unto a wise man,
which built his house upon a rock: and the rain
descended, and the floods came, and the winds
blew, and beat upon that house; and it fell not:
for it was founded upon a rock.*

Matthew 7:24, 25 KJV

*Every word of God is flawless; he is a shield to those
who take refuge in him.*

Proverbs 30:5 NIV

THE KNOWLEDGE OF THE SECRETS OF THE KINGDOM OF HEAVEN HAS BEEN GIVEN TO YOU....

—

Matthew 13:11 NIV

ETERNAL LIFE

But now being made free from sin, and become servants to God, ye have your fruit unto holiness, and the end everlasting life. For the wages of sin is death; but the gift of God is eternal life through Jesus Christ our Lord.

Romans 6:22, 23 KJV

Behold, I tell you a mystery; we will not all sleep, but we will all be changed, in a moment, in the twinkling of an eye, at the last trumpet; for the trumpet will sound, and the dead will be raised imperishable, and we will be changed. For this perishable must put on the imperishable, and this mortal must put on immortality. But when this perishable will have put on the imperishable, and this mortal will have put on immortality, then will come about the saying that is written, "DEATH IS SWALLOWED UP IN VICTORY. "O DEATH, WHERE IS YOUR VICTORY? O DEATH, WHERE IS YOUR STING?" The sting of death is sin, and the power of sin is the law; but thanks be to God, who gives us the victory through our Lord Jesus Christ.

1 Corinthians 15:51-57 NASB

TRULY, TRULY, I SAY TO YOU,
HE WHO HEARS MY WORD,
AND BELIEVES HIM WHO
SENT ME, HAS ETERNAL LIFE,
AND DOES NOT COME INTO
JUDGMENT, BUT HAS PASSED
OUT OF DEATH INTO LIFE.
TRULY, TRULY, I SAY TO YOU,
AN HOUR IS COMING AND
NOW IS, WHEN THE DEAD
WILL HEAR THE VOICE
OF THE SON OF GOD,
AND THOSE WHO HEAR
WILL LIVE.

—

John 5:24, 25 NASB